DATE DUE

Who Lives in a Wild, Wet Rain Forest?

Rachel Lynette

PowerKiDS press.

New York

For Alaina

Published in 2011 by The Rosen Publishing Group, Inc.
29 East 21st Street, New York, NY 10010

First Edition

Editor: Joanne Randolph
Book Design: Greg Tucker
Photo Researcher: Jessica Gerweck

Photo Credits: Cover, pp. 5, 6, 8, 10, 14, 15, 17, 18, 19, 20–21 Shutterstock.com; p. 4 © Kelli Patterson; p. 7 (top) © www.iStockphoto.com/Antonio Nunes; p. 7 (bottom) © www.iStockphoto.com/ Susan Flashman; p. 9 © www.iStockphoto.com/Roberto A. Sanchez; p. 11 Jeff Foott/Getty Images; pp. 12–13 © Juniors Bildarchiv/age fotostock; p. 16 James Balog/Getty Images; p. 22 Marcus Lyon/ Getty Images.

Library of Congress Cataloging-in-Publication Data

Lynette, Rachel.
  Who lives in a wild, wet rain forest? / Rachel Lynette. — 1st ed.
     p. cm. — (Exploring habitats)
  Includes index.
  ISBN 978-1-4488-0678-2 (library binding) — ISBN 978-1-4488-1283-7 (pbk.) —
ISBN 978-1-4488-1284-4 (6-pack)
  1. Rain forest animals—Juvenile literature. 2. Rain forest ecology—
Juvenile literature. I. Title.
  QL112.L94 2011
  591.734—dc22

                                   2010000423

Manufactured in the United States of America

CPSIA Compliance Information: Batch #WS10PK: For Further Information contact Rosen Publishing, New York, New York at 1-800-237-9932

Contents

What Is a Rain Forest?

If you were walking in a tropical rain forest, you would see plants everywhere. You would see animals, too. The air would feel very warm and **humid**. It is warm because it is near the **equator**.

This is a temperate rain forest in the state of Washington. Lots of moss grows from the tree branches in this forest.

The weather is always warm near the equator. A tropical rain forest is humid because it rains there almost every day. There are thousands of different kinds of plants and animals in a rain forest. In fact, there are more different kinds of plants and animals in a tropical rain forest than anywhere else on Earth!

4

There are temperate rain forests, too. Like tropical rain forests, temperate rain forests get lots of rain. However, the air is not as warm in temperate rain forests because they are not near the equator. This book is mostly about tropical rain forests.

Tropical rain forests, such as this one, are found in rainy places near the equator. Tropical plants grow in them.

The rain forest can be divided into four parts, or layers. The bottom layer is the forest floor. Because it is so dark in this layer, there are few plants. Lots of insects, arachnids, snakes, and large animals, such as armadillos and **peccaries**, live in this layer.

Emerald tree boas, like this one, wrap themselves around tree branches. When hunting, they hang their heads down to catch their food.

The next layer is the understory. Bushes, ferns, and young trees are part of the understory. Insects and amphibians, such as frogs and salamanders, live here. Jaguars and emerald tree boas also live in this leafy layer.

Here you can see the rain forest canopy. A few trees rise above the canopy, making up the emergent layer.

Above the understory is the canopy. The canopy is made up of the tops of trees. Birds, howler monkeys, and **sakis** live here. The emergent level is made up of the tall trees that grow above the canopy. Many small animals and birds, such as the harpy eagle, live in these high branches.

Peccaries look like wild pigs, but they are in their own family. Peccaries generally move through the rain forest in groups.

Plenty of Plants

A rain forest is a little like a **greenhouse**. Just like in a greenhouse, the warm, humid air helps the plants grow. More than two-thirds of the world's plants grow in tropical rain forests. All those plants are homes and food for animals.

Tree frogs often hide or live in the leaves of rain forest plants called bromeliads.

Colorful flowers make **pollen** for bees and butterflies. Monkeys swing on hanging vines and branches. They stop to snack on the trees' fruits and leaves.

One kind of plant that grows in tropical rain forests is the kapok tree. Tall kapok trees are part of the emergent layer. Many kinds of birds make their nests high in these trees' branches. People use the fiber from seedpods for many things, including stuffing pillows.

Banana trees grow in tropical rain forests. Rain forest animals, including bugs, birds, and people, eat the fruits.

Living Low

Many animals live on the forest floor. Insects, such as beetles and ants, eat leaves that fall to the ground. Army ants travel in huge **swarms** of more than 300,000 ants. They eat any insect or small animal that cannot get out of the swarm's way!

The rhinoceros beetle eats rotting fruit and sap from rain forest trees. Can you guess how this beetle got its name?

Snakes crawl over the forest floor. Lizards jump from log to log. Armadillos dig burrows in the forest floor and feast on all kinds of insects. Mongooses eat eggs and hunt for lizards, frogs, and other small animals.

Gorillas are at home on the forest floor, too. Even though gorillas weigh up to 500 pounds (227 kg), they eat only plants and insects. They live in groups, called troops.

This armadillo mother and her baby rest inside their burrow. Armadillos sleep for up to 16 hours each day, coming out in the morning and evening to eat insects.

The Giant Anaconda

Green anacondas make their homes in South American rain forests. They spend much of their time in the water, where they wait for animals to come for a drink. Anacondas eat wild pigs,

Green anacondas can go weeks or months without food after a big meal. There are many other kinds of anacondas, but they are all smaller than the green anaconda.

turtles, birds, deer, caimans, and even jaguars if they can catch them. They hunt at night and kill their prey by pulling the animals under water and drowning them. They can also squeeze them to death with their strong bodies.

Green anacondas are relatives of boa constrictors. They are the biggest snakes in the world. The longest green anaconda ever seen was more than 37 feet (11 m) long! That is about as long as a school bus.

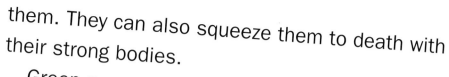

Lots of Life in the Understory

The understory is full of life. Many insects live in the trees. They become food for tree frogs and birds. Birds that live in the thick understory cannot fly long distances. They flit from branch to branch.

Fruit bats hang around in the understory trying to stay cool during the day. Some fruit bats have wings that are 6 feet (2 m) from tip to tip!

Many kinds of monkeys and apes live in the understory. Apes do not have tails, but monkeys do. They use their strong arms to swing from vine to vine. Orangutans can hold on to branches with their hands and their feet.

The capuchin monkey is one kind of monkey that lives in the branches of understory trees. This monkey lives in large groups of up to 35 monkeys. They eat fruit, insects, leaves, frogs, nuts, and small birds.

This baby orangutan holds on to a tree with its hands and feet while it eats. Mother orangutans give birth only once every eight years.

Tree-Loving Jaguars

Large cats often live in rain forests around the world as well. Tigers, jaguars, leopards, and pumas sleep in the trees during the day. At night they hunt for prey on the ground, in the water, or in the trees.

Here a jaguar rests in the branches of the understory.

Jaguars are the biggest of South America's big cats. Jaguars are not picky eaters. They hunt and eat wild pigs, deer, fish, and anything else they can find. They may wait for prey in the trees or on the ground.

South American people have admired jaguars' beauty and power for thousands of years. Even today, their skins are highly valued, which is why these rain forest hunters are **endangered**.

This jaguar has spotted some prey. The jaguar hides among the leaves on the forest floor as it waits for its chance to make a kill.

Sky High in the Treetops

Animals that live in the canopy and emergent layers of the rain forest spend their lives high in the trees. Monkeys use their tails to hold on to branches and vines. They eat fruits, seeds, leaves, and insects.

Pygmy marmosets eat mostly tree sap, but they also eat bugs, nectar, and fruit. When baby pygmy marmosets are born, their fathers take care of them.

The smallest monkey is the pygmy marmoset. It is so small it could easily fit in your hand! A small monkey may be eaten by a harpy eagle, which lives and hunts in the emergent layer. Other more colorful birds, such as macaws and toucans, live in the canopy.

Toucans are known for their long, sometimes colorful beaks. There are 40 kinds of toucans in South American and Central American rain forests.

They make their nests in the hollows of trees. Toucans use their large beaks to eat fruit that other animals would have a hard time reaching.

Red-eyed tree frogs hide in the rain forest canopy or understory during the day. At night they use their sticky tongues to catch bugs, such as crickets and flies.

Just Hanging Around

Sloths spend almost all their time hanging upside down in the rain forest canopy. They eat, sleep, move, and even have babies while hanging upside down from their strong hook-shaped **claws**.

Sloths eat leaves, buds, shoots, insects, and birds. Most of what they eat is leaves, though. It takes up to a month for the sloth to break down its food.

A sloth may spend its whole life in a single tree. Sloths move very slowly in the trees. On the ground, a sloth cannot even walk. It must pull itself along with its claws.

Sloths are great swimmers, though!

Even though sloths are brown, they can sometimes look green. That is because they often have **algae** growing in their fur. The algae keep them safe by making them blend into the tree's leaves. Sometimes sloths lick the algae for extra food.

Animals in Danger

Thousands of plants and animals live in rain forests. Sadly, people are cutting down rain forests to build farms and cities. People use the trees to build houses and furniture. These activities cause more **pollution**.

Trees in this rain forest in Brazil have been burned to clear the land for people to use.

Many rain forest animals cannot live in this polluted **environment**. People also hunt rain forest animals.

Many rain forest plants and animals cannot be found anywhere else in the world. How can we keep rain forests safe?

Glossary

algae (AL-jee) Plantlike living things without roots or stems.

claws (KLAWZ) The sharp parts of an animal's feet.

endangered (in-DAYN-jerd) In danger of no longer living.

environment (en-VY-ern-ment) All the living things and conditions of a place.

equator (ih-KWAY-tur) The imaginary line around Earth that separates it into two parts, northern and southern.

greenhouse (GREEN-hows) A building that traps heat from the Sun to help plants grow.

humid (HYOO-med) Wet.

peccaries (PEH-kuh-reez) Medium-sized, piglike mammals in North America and South America.

pollen (PAH-lin) A yellow dust made by the male parts of flowers.

pollution (puh-LOO-shun) Manmade waste that hurts Earth's air, land, or water.

sakis (SAK-eez) New World monkeys of the genus *Pithecia*.

swarms (SWORMZ) Large numbers of insects that are often moving.

Index

Web Sites

Due to the changing nature of Internet links, PowerKids Press has developed an online list of Web sites related to the subject of this book. This site is updated regularly. Please use this link to access the list:
www.powerkidslinks.com/explore/wwrf/